Contents

Acknowledgments

This book has been compiled with the co-operation of several organisations, including other government departments and agencies. The editor would like to thank all those who have contributed their comments, and in particular the Foreign and Commonwealth Office (especially the Overseas Development Administration), the Commonwealth Secretariat, the British Council, the Crown Agents, the BBC World Service, Oxfam, the Save the Children Fund, Christian Aid and the Intermediate Technology Development Group.

Photograph Credits
Photographs refer to pages 1–4 of the illustration section: the Commonwealth Development Corporation p. 1 (top and bottom); United Nations Development Programme p. 2 (centre); the Overseas development Administration p. 2 (top); Christian Aid p. 3 (top), p. 4 (centre); Oxfam p. 3 (centre); Intermediate Technology Development Group p. 3 (bottom), p. 4 (top); Voluntary Services Overseas p. 4 (bottom).

THE ANNUAL PICTURE

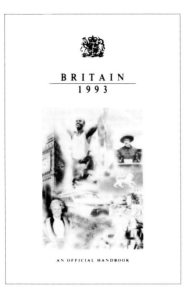

BRITAIN
1993

AN OFFICIAL HANDBOOK

BRITAIN HANDBOOK

The annual picture of Britain is provided by *Britain: An Official Handbook* - the forty-fourth edition will be published early in 1993. It is the unrivalled reference book about Britain, packed with information and statistics on every facet of British life.

With a circulation of over 20,000 worldwide, it is essential for libraries, educational institutions, business organisations and individuals needing easy access to reliable and up-to-date information, and is supported in this role by its sister publication, *Current Affairs: A Monthly Survey*.

Approx. 500 pages; 24 pages of colour illustrations; 16 maps; diagrams and tables throughout the text; and a statistical section. Price £19·50.

Buyers of Britain 1993: An Official Handbook *have the opportunity of a year's subscription to* Current Affairs *at 25 per cent off the published price of £35·80. They will also have the option of renewing their subscription next year at the same discount. Details in each copy of* Handbook, *from HMSO Publications Centre and at HMSO bookshops (see back of title page).*

Britain and Africa

London: H M S O

Researched and written by Reference Services,
Central Office of Information.

© Crown copyright 1993
Applications for reproduction should be made to HMSO.
First published 1993

ISBN 0 11 701731 0

HMSO

HMSO publications are available from:

HMSO Publications Centre
(Mail, fax and telephone orders only)
PO Box 276, London SW8 5DT
Telephone orders 071-873 9090
General enquiries 071-873 0011
(queuing system in operation for both numbers)
Fax orders 071-873 8200

HMSO Bookshops
49 High Holborn, London WC1V 6HB   071-873 0011
Fax 071-873 8200 (counter service only)
258 Broad Street, Birmingham B1 2HE   021-643 3740   Fax 021-643 6510
Southey House, 33 Wine Street, Bristol BS1 2BQ
0272 264306   Fax 0272 294515
9-21 Princess Street, Manchester M60 8AS   061-834 7201   Fax 061-833 0634
16 Arthur Street, Belfast BT1 4GD   0232 238451   Fax 0232 235401
71 Lothian Road, Edinburgh EH3 9AZ   031-228 4181   Fax 031-229 2734

HMSO's Accredited Agents
(see Yellow Pages)

and through good booksellers

Introduction

Links between Britain and Africa have existed for over four centuries, and Britain has been actively involved in the continent's development since the nineteenth century. Through the period of British administration that began at that time, a particularly close relationship was formed with a number of African countries; and as independent states they inherited a number of British institutions and practices, the basis of a modern economic sector and the medium of the English language.

The development of these countries continues to be of concern to Britain, which supports their efforts to achieve a sustained reduction in poverty while also promoting economic growth through economic reform and well-designed development projects. Although most of British aid in Africa goes to Commonwealth countries, aid to non-Commonwealth countries is significant. While much effort has to be spent to combat the drought and other emergencies affecting most of the African continent, Britain also recognises the value of long-term development assistance, in particular, by investing in community development projects and providing technical aid.

This book describes briefly Britain's historical links with Africa and examines aspects of British aid and the various institutions (including the International Monetary Fund and the World Bank, the United Nations, the Commonwealth Development Corporation, and the British Council) which dispense this aid. Other questions discussed include the increasing use of good-government assistance to African countries implementing economic reform programmes; the importance of voluntary societies in focusing emergency and refugee relief; and the role of the Commonwealth.

Further information on developments in Britain's relations with Africa is contained in *Current Affairs – A Monthly Survey*, published by HMSO.

History

Britain has links with Africa which can be traced back to the 1500s, when the first voyages were made by British traders to the Guinea coast of West Africa. Gold dust, ivory and pepper were among the commodities exchanged for cloth, metal utensils and other goods. These traders were followed later by a number of British explorers and then by Christian missions.

The existence of slavery and the slave trade provoked a humanitarian campaign which resulted in the British Parliament abolishing first the slave trade in 1807 and then slavery itself in all British possessions in 1834. In East Africa, Britain's interest was limited, until the late nineteenth century, to putting an end to the operations of Arab slave-traders.

Formal connection with Africa only took place during the later nineteenth century, since British Governments themselves were reluctant to extend responsibilities to Africa; even when territorial claims were made (partly because of rivalry with other European countries) direct responsibility for administration was often left to British trading companies. It was only after a conference of European powers in 1884–85, which decided that sovereignty had to depend on effective occupation, that a gradual extension of Britain's authority took place.

Strategic considerations, backed by humanitarian pressures, were therefore as important as commercial considerations in dictating the extension of Britain's responsibilities in Africa. The volume of trade with Africa in the Victorian era was comparatively small. However, although the period of effective British administration was brief (about 60 years, in most cases), it helped to create many of the basic political and economic structures required by modern states, and provided a foundation on which to build after independence.

The creation of basic infrastructure included:

—the development of 2,000 miles of railways in Nigeria, 35,000 miles of roads in East Africa and 29,300 miles of roads in West Africa;

—the creation of port facilities; and

—the construction of dams and hydroelectric schemes.

After 1945 Britain decided to guide its dependent territories towards self-government and independence on terms designed to establish a modern system of government which included:

—representative parliamentary and local government institutions;

—an established public service;

—an independent judiciary; and

—education and health services.

In Africa, this policy meant that most of the dependent territories there gained independence within 12 years (1956 to 1968); almost all the new states chose to join the Commonwealth.

The first African country achieved independence from Britain in 1957 when the Gold Coast and British Togoland became Ghana. During the 1960s other countries followed suit: Nigeria (1960), Sierra Leone and Tanzania (1961).[1] Uganda (1962), Kenya (1963), Malawi and Zambia (1964), The Gambia (1965), Botswana

[1]After gaining independence in 1961 and 1963 respectively, Tanganyika and Zanzibar combined to form the United Republic of Tanganyika and Zanzibar (renamed Tanzania).

and Lesotho (1966), and Mauritius and Swaziland (1968). The Seychelles became an independent republic within the Commonwealth in 1976, while Zimbabwe also gained independence as a republic and chose Commonwealth membership in 1980.

Other territories which achieved independence were: the Sudan (a British-French condominium); the British Cameroons, part of which joined Nigeria and part the Republic of Cameroon; and the British Somaliland Protectorate, which became part of Somalia. After a long-drawn out dispute involving the United Nations and South Africa, Namibia became independent as a republic, joining the Commonwealth in 1990.

British Aid Policy

Africa is the largest element of Britain's aid expenditure—over 37 per cent of bilateral aid and nearly 40 per cent of multilateral aid in 1990. A total of over £1,800 million on aid, with over 45 per cent of bilateral aid going to Africa, is planned for 1991–92. The reasons for this concentration have been the long-term economic, social and political problems faced by African countries, including:

—a continuing decline in per capita income;

—a growth of population that has doubled in 25 years; and

—the effects of natural disasters (such as drought), and civil wars.

British Policy

Britain focuses its aid on the poorest countries in ways which are the most likely to achieve a sustained reduction in poverty. About 76 per cent of British bilateral aid directly allocated goes to countries with average incomes of less than $700 per head, with 70 per cent to the poorest 50 countries. In Africa, about 25 per cent of Britain's long-term development aid promotes renewable natural resources.

Britain is alleviating poverty by:

—promoting economic growth through support for economic reform and well-designed development projects;

—paying attention to the income and welfare of poor people when designing economic reform programmes and individual projects; and

—directing increasing amounts of aid through non-government
organisations, which are often best placed to undertake projects
in the poorest communities.

Good Government

Britain believes that economic growth depends on market
economies, and open and effective government. Referring to the
link between good government and development in a speech in
June 1990, the Foreign and Commonwealth Secretary, Mr Douglas
Hurd, pointed out that aid programmes had to take account of
countries' records on government. Some of the components of
good government were listed by Lady Chalker, the Minister for
Overseas Development, in June 1991. These are:

—sound economic and social policies, free markets and an
enhanced role for the private sector, the provision of essential
services and curbs on military expenditure;

—competence of government, involving the need to train civil
servants to improve administrative capacity and accountability;

—pluralistic political systems which are open and accountable,
reduce political interference and corruption, and maintain a free
press; and

—respect for human rights and the rule of law.

In a speech to the Southern Africa Association in February
1992, Lady Chalker said that Britain wanted its aid to be effective.
It was not for donors to try to impose a list of criteria for good government since the impulse had to come from within and this was

happening more and more.[2] 'African governments must decide for themselves exactly how to interpret good government, and put it to work. But in the few cases where they are not doing so at all, we have to decide whether we should continue giving development aid, when there are so many who could make better use of our help . . . in the long run, it is sound and fully accountable governments which will produce stability and economic growth, not repressive or corrupt ones.'

The question of good government has also been the subject of a number of reports by international organisations, for instance a report by the World Bank in 1989 on long-term perspectives in Africa. In the programme of action adopted by the second UN Conference on the Least Developed Countries in 1990, it was agreed that 'Good governance is essential for economic and social progress for all countries.' In December 1991, the Development Assistance Committee (DAC) of the Organisation for Economic Co-operation and Development (OECD) highlighted democratisation, the respect of human rights and good governance as basic conditions for achieving sustainable development. The International Monetary Fund (IMF) is also investigating the effects of excessive military spending on its economic reform programmes. There is recognition within Africa of the link between improved governance and accountability and successful long-term development.

---

[2]In addition to the democratic reforms undertaken in South Africa (see pp. 46–7), demands for multi-party elections have been recognised elsewhere in Africa: elections have been held in Benin, Cameroon and Zambia (where a new government was democratically elected in 1991); multi-party elections have been promised in other African countries, including Angola, Ghana, Guinea-Bissau, Kenya, Lesotho, the Seychelles and Tanzania. In Nigeria a change to a civil administration is planned to take place in 1993.

At its Heads of Government Meeting in Harare in October 1991, the Commonwealth stressed the need, among other priorities, to protect and promote:

—democracy, the rule of law and the independence of the judiciary, and just and honest government;

—fundamental human rights, including equal rights and opportunities for all citizens regardless of race, colour, creed or political belief;

—provision of universal access to education; and

—a stable international economic framework and sound economic management that recognises the central role of the market economy.

Good Government Assistance
Britain spent about £30 million during 1991–92 on projects designed to encourage good government in over 50 countries (including many in Africa) in the fields of:

—public administration, public expenditure management and legal affairs; and

—processes and institutions designed to promote democratic and pluralistic structures, a free press and human rights.

Britain's bilateral projects designed to improve government include:

—the development of local government in the central district of Zambia;

—training of Zimbabwean police;

—assisting city councils in Malawi;

—helping civil service reform in Ghana;

—providing judges in Uganda;

—improving financial management in central government and strengthening local government in Tanzania; and

—training senior provincial administrators in Kenya.

New measures have also been announced to help South Africa along the road to non-racial democracy, such as public administration courses for black South Africans (see pp. 48–9).

Britain is also providing balance-of-payments support for countries implementing IMF-approved economic reform programmes via the European Community (EC) and other multilateral organisations. Most of the support given in 1989 and 1990—around £260 million—was to countries in sub-Saharan Africa.

Debt Support

Many of the poorest countries in Africa—including many Commonwealth states—have heavy and unsustainable debts to governments.

Britain is encouraging other government creditors to support its proposals to reduce the debt owed by these states. In a scheme introduced in 1978, Britain has helped to remove the burden of outstanding aid loans made to the poorest countries by waiving its claim to further repayments. Britain has written off aid debts worth £290 million for 16 African countries.

Britain was the first major creditor to propose that debt concessions should be extended to the non-aid debts owed to governments (owed mainly to export credit agencies). This led to international agreement at the Toronto Economic Summit in 1988, from which 18 African countries have benefited.

At the Trinidad Commonwealth Finance Ministers' Conference in 1990, Britain announced new proposals on debt relief. These proposals would mean that debts of the poorest countries to governments would be reduced by two-thirds, and the remainder would be repayable over 25 years provided that they pursue economic reform programmes. Between December 1991 and April 1992, five countries, including Benin and Tanzania, benefited from the terms arranged in Trinidad. Britain continues to press other government creditors to offer further relief for those countries that need it.

In addition, Britain provides balance-of-payments assistance via the World Bank's Special Programme of Assistance (SPA) to low-income, debt-distressed sub-Saharan African countries.

British Aid

Britain's gross public expenditure on overseas aid in 1990 was £1,725 million. Table 1 shows the breakdown of bilateral and multilateral aid during 1990.

Table 1: Gross Public Expenditure on Overseas Aid 1990

Bilateral Aid by Region	£m	%
Africa, North of Sahara	20	1.2
Africa, South of Sahara	369	21.4
Caribbean	69	4.0
Latin America	25	1.4
Middle East	18	1.1
Asia, South	227	13.2
Asia, Far East	85	4.9
Europe	5	0.3
Pacific (Oceania)	28	1.6
Unallocable	196	11.3
Total	**1042**	**60.4**
Multilateral Aid		
European Community	333	19.3
World Bank Group	184	10.6
UN and other	166	9.7
Total	**683**	**39.6**
Total Gross Aid	**1725**	**100**

Bilateral Aid

In 1990 Britain gave £389 million (of £1,042 million) in bilateral aid to Africa. The main recipients of this aid were Kenya (£44 million), Malawi (£37 million), Mozambique (£25 million), Zambia (£25 million), Uganda (£24 million), Tanzania (£23 million), Sudan (£21 million), Zimbabwe (£21 million), Ethiopia (£20 million) and Ghana (£20 million).

A number of Commonwealth African countries also received substantial programme-aid from Britain agreed during 1990 for their economic reform programmes, including Nigeria (£25 million), Zambia (£30 million), Ghana (£10 million), and Uganda (£10 million).

Technical Co-operation

Technical co-operation is the transfer of specialised knowledge and skills from country to country, and the provision of equipment and supplies. Increasingly, British technical co-operation is being used to support economic reforms in African countries, including help with policies designed to give people incentives to raise output and incomes. This assistance includes:

—Overseas Development Administration (ODA) financed work on agricultural policies in Tanzania;

—work in the financial sector in Ghana and Tanzania; and

—assistance for tax reform in Kenya, The Gambia, Uganda and other countries which will raise the financial resources available to governments.

Britain is also helping governments to improve the management of resources in the public sector, such as:

—assistance with budgetary reform (Ghana);

—programmes of training and other institutional support in major public projects such as Kenya Railways and Maputo Port; and

—assistance in the reform of the civil service (The Gambia and Ghana).

To ensure that these reforms are sustainable, Britain is providing training programmes (over £40 million in 1990) in Britain and overseas, as well as local training courses. Many of these technical awards are related to ODA-financed aid activities.

In 1985 churches and schools in Lesotho and Wales established a link between their respective countries. As part of a population health and nutrition project the ODA, acting for Lesotho, arranged in 1990 a two-year management consultancy and training contract with a local authority in Wales, providing work with local managers at the main hospital in Maseru, the capital of Lesotho, and assisting the Ministry of Health in the development of expertise in manpower planning and human resources.

Project Aid

Britain's project-aid in Africa, which was £63 million in 1990, focuses on rehabilitation of essential infrastructure such as roads, railways, and electrical power. To increase the electrical supply to Uganda, Britain is rehabilitating the Owen Falls hydroelectric power-station in Uganda; one of the purposes of this project is to increase the rating of the power-station from 150 MW to 180 MW without increasing the flow of water. A smaller station is being rehabilitated in Ghana.

Other projects supported by Britain include equipment and material as part of British-funded construction of highways in

Tanzania and Kenya, bridges in The Gambia and Swaziland, and clean water supply and sanitation (Ghana).

Increasingly, Britain gives attention to direct poverty-reducing projects. Some of these aim to raise income directly, for example, supporting small-scale enterprises in Ghana and Kenya or, through the British contribution to agricultural research in Zimbabwe, solving problems regarding poverty in communal areas. In Tanzania, an ODA-supported Mbeya pilot nutrition project aims to help with women's income-generation support; the extra income for the families can then improve the nutrition of children in the area.

Other projects try to enhance living standards and raise productive potential by improving access to clean water and basic health—for example, three projects in Ghana for waste disposal, water supplies, and basic health worth £8 million.

Multilateral Aid

In 1990 about 40 per cent of British aid was channelled through the World Bank, the European Community, the United Nations (UN) agencies and the regional development banks.

European Community Aid

As a member of the European Community (EC), Britain gave more than £330 million to its aid programmes to Africa in 1990. The Community and its member states are among the main sources of official aid for the developing countries. Although the bulk of this is given bilaterally by member states, the Community as a whole provides aid through the Lomé Convention and programmes for non-associated developing countries. The amount of Community aid from the seventh European Development Fund (EDF)—which provided almost a half of EC aid-expenditure in 1989—is about £8,500 million for the five years to 1995, with Britain contributing £1,300 million. Of the £8,500 million, some £800 million is in the form of loans from the European Investment Bank.

The EDF also has a structural adjustment facility to help developing countries which are participating in IMF/World Bank economic reform programmes; 30 developing countries are eligible to use grants from this facility, which has resources of about £775 million. The objectives are:

—to control inflation;

—to restore the access to imports needed for growth; and

—to restore the capacity to meet the basic needs of the population, and to raise productivity and income.

The Lomé Convention provides for increased consultation between the Community and each developing state to ensure that aid is put to the best possible use within the context of the recipient country's own policies. Emphasis is placed on:

—agriculture and food production;

—improving rural productivity and the rational exploitation of plant and animal resources;

—raising rural incomes and standards of living;

—developing local processing of agricultural produce;

—ensuring a better balance between food and export crops; and

—encouraging agricultural research.

Priority is also being given to measures to:

—combat drought and desertification; and

—increase the contribution of the fishing industry to food supply (helping to buy fishing boats and equipment, and giving advice on the processing and marketing of fish products).

The Community's food aid programme for developing countries (some £413 million in 1991) is designed to be an effective instrument of development policy rather than a short-term expedient for the disposal of food surpluses.

World Bank Group

Britain is a member of the World Bank and the International Development Association (IDA), which is the World Bank's interest-free loans facility for poorer developing countries. The IDA lends interest-free money over longer repayment periods (40 years plus a 10-year grace period) to countries whose per capita gross national product (GNP) is below $700. Britain's contribution to the IDA's ninth replenishment for the years 1991 to 1993 is a commitment of £619 million towards a total of $15,500 million.

Economic Reform Programmes

Britain recognises the importance of assisting African countries in their implementation of economic reform programmes. For example, Britain made available £250 million for the first phase of the World Bank's Special Programme of Assistance (SPA), which mobilises balance-of-payment programmes in support of economic reforms in sub-Saharan countries that have low incomes and large debts. Britain has made an increased pledge of £300 million to Phase II (1991–93), about 10 per cent of the total of such bilateral commitments.

Britain is also the largest contributor—some £327 million over 14 years—to the Enhanced Structural Adjustment Facility of the International Monetary Fund (IMF) which is used to lend money on highly concessional terms to the poorest countries pursuing economic reforms.

Altogether 28 African countries are implementing World Bank/IMF reform programmes; a number of Commonwealth countries in Africa have received programme pledges from Britain including £40 million to Zambia, £17 million to Tanzania, and £15 million to Uganda. Ghana also received £10 million from Britain for balance-of-payment support.

United Nations Agencies
African countries benefit from Britain's contributions to the United Nations and its development activities. One of the UN's main aims is to promote economic and social advance by giving aid to poor countries. This amounted to $6,000 million in 1990.

In 1991 Britain contributed more than £120 million to the various UN agencies. It has encouraged moves to concentrate resources on the poorer countries and communities in the developing world. It also supports effective aid co-ordination to avoid unnecessary duplication by the various agencies.

In 1991 Britain gave £28 million to the UN Development Programme, which is the central funding and co-ordinating body for UN technical co-operation. Contributions were also made to the UN Children's Fund (£9 million), the UN High Commissioner for Refugees (UNHCR—£23.5 million), the UN Population Fund (£10.5 million), and the Food and Agriculture Organisation (FAO—£3 million). In addition, some 14.1 million was given to the World Health Organisation (WHO).

Britain fully supports the work of the World Health Organisation (WHO) in co-ordinating international efforts to prevent and control AIDS (Acquired Immune Deficiency Syndrome). Britain has contributed £21.4 million to the WHO Global Programme on AIDS and is the third largest donor. It has also agreed to give £7.3 million through the WHO for medium-term AIDS control plans in Africa and the Caribbean, and is giving a grant of £3 million over six years to the International Planned Parenthood Federation to help family planning associations introduce information and counselling services on AIDS.

Regional Development Banks
Regional development banks have been growing in importance in providing funds for developing countries. Commitments in 1990 were $11,300 million.

African Development Bank
Britain contributed £13 million to the resources of the African Development Bank (ADB) and its African Development Fund (ADF) in 1990.

Britain is a founder member of the Bank, set up in 1973 to contribute to the economic development and social progress of its regional members, and which now has 25 non-African member states. The Fund—part of the Bank—lends money on concessional terms. The Bank replenishment covers 1991–93 and is approximately £1,800 million; Britain's share of this sum is £71.9 million.

During the negotiations for the 1991–93 round, it was agreed that allocation of resources had to be based more on the performance of the borrowing countries, and that these resources should go to programmes and projects where they would be used most effectively. The Fund concentrates on those borrowing countries which pursue sound economic policies by giving its resources to

African countries that are implementing adjustment programmes supported by the IMF and the World Bank.

Charities in Africa

There are about 110 British voluntary aid agencies involved in development work overseas.

The Government made over £88 million available to these organisations in 1990–91. About half of this contribution was spent on longer-term development and half on disaster and other emergency relief work.

Long Term Development

The voluntary agencies, which received government grants for more than 1,380 selected development projects during 1991–92, work in close partnership with local groups and organisations in the countries concerned. Projects focus on primary health care, prevention of AIDS, clean water supply, community development, smallholder agriculture, income-generation schemes, and the environment. Projects that involve women are also highlighted by voluntary agencies.

The Save the Children Fund (SCF) continued its support for a programme to restore government health services in two West Nile counties in Uganda after 15 years of civil war; also in Uganda the SCF spent £1.9 million during 1990–91 on medical projects such as assistance on an expanded programme of immunisation, on services for disabled children, and on an AIDS prevention and control programme. Comic Relief donated over £4.6 million for long-term and emergency work by SCF in 14 countries in Africa. In addition, Comic Relief launched Red Nose Day in March 1991, raising a further £20 million, two-thirds of which went towards the work of Oxfam, SCF and other agencies in Africa.

In Uganda, Oxfam funded several community health, clean water supply and agricultural initiatives in 1991. These included the marketing of traditional honey to outlets in the capital, Kampala, and the renewal of the water supply system to Kagando hospital and the local community of some 12,000 people.

Also in Uganda, Christian Aid assisted women to establish small-scale businesses by funding a finance and credit trust; this trust provides loans, for example, for poultry-keeping, shoe-making and horticulture. In Senegal, Christian Aid is funding cereal banks which buy grain from peasant farmers above the market price during harvest time; in the dry season, grain can be bought back at below the higher market price.

In Egypt Oxfam runs a credit scheme making loans to women for income-generating projects ranging from selling fruit and vegetables outside their homes to collecting and grading waste material for resale merchants.

In the Ziway region of Ethiopia, the Catholic Fund for Overseas Development (CAFOD) is working with farmers' associations to plant forests, improve water supplies and provide irrigated vegetable gardens. In Eritrea, the charity has improved the food production system by supplying plough animals, seeds, tools, advice and expertise; it also set up food-for-work schemes as well as providing facilities that have improved the way of life of over 5,000 households. In Tanzania, where 70 per cent of the country's forests has been lost over 50 years, CAFOD emphasises programmes which protect the environment, including giving grants to forestry projects. CAFOD-supported schemes in Kenya have involved food production, adult education, health, water and soil conservation, a veterinary programme and small businesses.

A British charity, Wateraid, has introduced a new training initiative to strengthen local organisations in developing countries; in 1990–91 the charity spent £2.5 million on rural water projects in Sierra Leone, Uganda, Kenya, Tanzania, Ghana, Ethiopia and The Gambia.

Emergency Aid

Despite focusing primarily on long-term development work, British voluntary societies, whose field officers are often the only reliable source of information about the effects of disasters in remote areas, have long been providers of emergency relief. A substantial proportion of their total revenue is used in this way.

The main voluntary agencies concerned in emergency relief are the British Red Cross, CAFOD, Christian Aid, Oxfam, and SCF. With Action Aid and Help the Aged, they form the Disaster Emergency Committee, which mounts national appeals for major overseas disasters. Like many others, these charities liaise closely with, and receive funds from, the ODA's Disaster Unit.

In 1991, the British Red Cross spent £29.5 million on disaster relief as against £12 million in 1990. About 45 per cent of Oxfam's expenditure in 1990–91, some £20.4 million, was on emergencies, while more than £9 million of Christian Aid's overseas expenditure of £26.8 million was directed to emergencies and assistance to refugees. Supported by public appeals, including the 'Crisis in Africa' appeal which brought in £1.6 million, Christian Aid was able to continue to provide trucks, spare parts, water-drilling equipment and food to people from Mozambique to Eritrea and from Somalia to Sierra Leone.

Oxfam and SCF jointly ran relief food convoys in Tigray, Ethiopia and Eritrea and, when a gap in the flow of aid was threatened, Oxfam raised more than £1 million for food for 350,000 people in Ethiopia and Sudan. In Mozambique, Oxfam provided seeds, tools and clothing to hundreds of thousands of people caught up in the civil war there. In Liberia, the charity sent in experts on water and nutrition, while in Somalia an Oxfam water team visited towns devastated by war.

There are nearly 1 million refugees seeking shelter in Malawi from the civil war in neighbouring Mozambique; about half of these are under 15 years of age. With the United Nations High Commissioner for Refugees, the SCF helped to supply refugees and neighbouring communities with clean water, as well as training refugees in water pump maintenance. The SCF also assisted with nutritional surveys of Malawian and Mozambican children, helping to control common infectious diseases and training local health workers. In addition to providing health care and nutrition for refugees, the SCF's work in Ethiopia in 1991 also included support for mother-and-child health services; and immunisation programmes.

In 1991 more than 80 per cent (£8.6 million) of CAFOD's emergency expenditure went to relief operations in Africa. In Ethiopia, CAFOD's main area of operation, the charity disbursed 15,000 tonnes of food provided by the British Government; it also organised another 6,000 tonnes of food purchased locally for distribution in Tigray.

Joint Funding Scheme

Support for the development operations overseas of non-governmental organisations (NGOs) is provided by the Joint Funding Scheme (JFS), in which the Government provides grants of up to 50 per cent of agreed long-term development projects. In 1991–92 government assistance under this scheme was over £23 million; a 22 per cent increase in the JFS for 1992–93 (£28 million) has been agreed.

Block grants to finance projects are provided to five agencies—the Catholic Fund for Overseas Development, Christian Aid, Oxfam, Save the Children Fund, and the World Wide Fund for Nature. During 1990–91 nearly half of the countries in which JFS projects were implemented were African.

The ODA dispensed further grants to charities during the year for particular emergency needs and long term programmes. The SCF, for example, spent £21.7 million (out of a total of £36.4 million) on various programmes in Africa. Part of this expenditure was covered by its block grant of £3 million, but the Fund also received further Government assistance of more than £6.6 million, ranging from:

—£1 million for emergency relief in Sudan;

—£100,000 to provide relief for refugees during civil strife in Liberia;

—£63,000 worth of supplementary food and medicines for Somalia; and

—£580,000 to provide food relief in Tigray and Eritrea.

In 1991, the Fund launched its 'Skip Lunch—Save a Life' appeal which raised £5 million for famine relief for 27 million people in Ethiopia, Sudan, Somalia, Mozambique, Malawi, Angola and Liberia.

Volunteers

Britain's volunteer recruiting agencies receive up to 90 per cent of funding from the ODA. Suitably qualified people are sent to work on development projects overseas—mainly training teachers and nurses, setting up agricultural extension programmes, and advising on marketing and accountancy—in response to requests from governments and organisations. Four main recruiting agencies are Voluntary Services Overseas (VSO), International Co-operation for Development, Skillshare Africa, and the United Nations Association International Service.

At the end of 1990 there were nearly 1,500 volunteers in at least 50 countries; about half of them in Commonwealth countries. The voluntary recruiting agencies received £15.8 million from the Government in 1991–92; this grant is being increased by £2 million in 1992–93.

In 1992 VSO had more than 1,500 volunteers overseas, half of them in Africa. About half of the VSO volunteers in Ghana (53) work as secondary school teachers and tutors in teacher training colleges, while in Kenya volunteers are involved in secondary school education and youth training initiatives as well as low-cost building, hand-tool production and small-enterprise initiatives. The health sector is the main focus of VSO activity in Malawi, with volunteers providing paramedical training and rehabilitation work in health posts and in refugee camps, where some 900,000 Mozambicans now live.

In Nigeria VSO volunteers are involved in education, health and agriculture, and help to increase self-reliance by teaching 'introductory technology' to junior secondary-school students. They also provide in-service training of instructors or serve as technical trainers in vocational colleges and as agricultural mechanics. To bridge essential skill gaps in Zambia, VSO is providing accountants, business managers, appropriate technologists and computer programmers to support and train in local enterprises; doctors, nurses, pharmacists, laboratory technicians and occupational therapists are involved in direct training or work at community level.

VSO's biggest programme in Africa is in Kenya, with 122 volunteers. There are 112 volunteers in Zimbabwe, of whom over half are teachers, teacher-trainers or otherwise involved in education.

Other Non-governmental Organisations

The ODA also assists the Intermediate Technology Development Group (ITDG). With experience of working in more than 60 countries and with 50 development organisations overseas, this organisation helps to develop and to introduce in developing countries appropriate small-scale technologies which will increase the income and skills of the poorer sections of the community. In 1990–91, ITDG's income was £5.8 million, with over £3 million coming from the ODA.

The Group is involved in schemes in Sudan, Kenya, Malawi and Zimbabwe. In western Kenya, it has been providing training and technical support to help six women's groups to make and sell fuel-efficient stoves; the first group was trained in 1988 and now produces more than 1,000 stoves a month. As part of an Oxfam project, ITDG is working with local herder groups in north Kenya, to develop ways to catch and store rainwater for millet gardening. A new phase has now started with the introduction of animal health techniques and improved access to medicines for their livestock. Other projects throughout Kenya are helping livestock owners to increase their understanding of animal husbandry and training people in animal first-aid.

In Zimbabwe, ITDG is supporting small-scale mining which provides an important source of income in rural areas. In addition to exploiting precious metals, the activity is also a source of many basic products for the building industry. Other schemes include training Mozambican exiles in Zimbabwe in carpentry and black-smithing as part of a Norwegian People's Aid project to promote useful trades amongst Mozambican refugees.

The ITDG is also co-ordinating seminars on 'Do it Herself', a study of women's role in technical innovations in Asia, Africa and Latin America; at a seminar held in Harare, Zimbabwe, in September 1991, researchers from eight African countries present-ed case studies of women's knowledge of and innovation in food-cycle technologies.

Humanitarian Aid

Humanitarian Relief

A quarter of Africa's population receive less than 80 per cent of their daily food needs, while 29 million people in 26 countries of sub-Saharan Africa are under threat from famine. All ten countries of southern Africa are suffering from the worst drought this century. Even traditionally surplus-food producers such as South Africa and Zimbabwe will have to import maize during 1992. The shortfall in other states in the region ranges from 42 per cent (Angola) to more than 90 per cent (Botswana and Mozambique), according to the UN World Food Programme. Malawi is likely to produce enough food for its indigenous population, but not for the refugees sheltering there.

The crisis is deepened by environmental factors, in particular climate change, soil, coastal and forestry erosion (most evident, for example, in the southerly advance of the Sahara desert), and high population growth rates (which are double the normal growth of food output). In addition, economic mismanagement, political repression, abuse of civil rights and civil war in some countries are barriers to effective aid.

Since the beginning of 1989 Britain has committed:

—at least £36 million to alleviate the plight of Africa's 6 million refugees, largely through support for the UN High Commissioner for Refugees; and

—£225 million, including its share of European Community help, in emergency assistance to alleviate famine in Africa.

Since September 1990, some £107 million (£30 million via the European Community, 185,000 tonnes of bilateral food aid, and £7 million of seeds, tools, transport and supplementary food) has been provided by Britain to countries in the Horn of Africa.

Table 2: Britain's Emergency Aid to the Horn of Africa

(£m)

Country	1989	1990	1991	Total
Sudan	15.228	14.129	27.065	56.422
Ethiopia	21.131	36.268	32.457	89.856
Liberia	–	3.608	3.366	6.974
Angola	2.268	2.630	2.995	7.889
Mozambique	13.830	18.515	7.310	39.655
Somalia	2.020	1.000	6.553	9.573
Horn of Africa	–	–	9.437	9.437
Africa	–	–	5.000	5.000
Total	**54.477**	**76.150**	**94.183**	**224.806**

Britain is providing a further £12 million of food aid (45,000 tonnes) and £11 million of relief assistance to Somalia, Sudan, Ethiopia/Eritrea. This represents its contribution to a $600 million UN special emergency programme for the Horn of Africa aimed at feeding 23 million people at risk there. The food will be distributed by the World Food Programme and British NGOs; of the relief aid, £5 million will be used for UNHCR activities in the Horn of Africa and £6 million to support humanitarian work by British voluntary agencies working in the region. Over £2 million of food aid was channelled through the International Committee of the Red Cross (ICRC) for its emergency feeding programme in southern and central Somalia. In March and April 1992 Britain pledged £30 million worth of aid to southern African countries to cope with the problems caused by the continuing drought there. This aid package involves:

—£17.5 million in balance-of-payments aid to Zambia and Zimbabwe to enable them to import essential food;

—up to 30,000 tonnes of aid food for Mozambique and 5,000 tonnes for Mozambican refugees in Malawi; and

—£2.5 million for voluntary agency activities for drought relief. Britain is also offering technical assistance for associated problems, for example, logistics and distribution management.

Other British assistance has included some £4.1 million in humanitarian aid to Liberia and to neighbouring countries where Liberians sought refuge from civil war in 1990; more recently, over £3.5 million of humanitarian aid has been sent to Somalia to provide medical assistance and food distribution to victims of civil war in that country, while £24 million was pledged in 1992.

The ODA's Disaster Unit co-ordinates Britain's official bilateral disaster aid. Much of this is channelled through voluntary agencies, such as Oxfam, the SCF and Christian Aid, which also raise funds through public appeals (see pp. 23–4). Britain is adding to its range of relief options a new plan to allow it to send personnel for short-term assignments when specific needs arise.

In 1991 the British and German Governments stimulated EC proposals to strengthen the United Nations' response to humanitarian emergencies. Britain believes that the UN should be ready to intervene in cases of acute emergency and to offer help to a host government without waiting for a request. The UN adopted these proposals and in May 1992 appointed an undersecretary-general for humanitarian affairs, able to deal directly with heads of government. The new official is responsible for giving a clear direction to co-ordinated international relief and controls a new emergency fund (to which Britain contributed the first $5 million) for relief to be sent within 24 hours.

Trade

Trade is vital to the economies of African countries. For about half of these, a few resources—raw materials such as copper and oil and/or cash crops (cotton, cocoa, coffee or tea)—still account for around 90 per cent of their export earnings. Through diversification, sub-Saharan Africa increased its manufactured exports by nearly 6 per cent a year between 1980 and 1987. Trade between countries in the Third World has also increased: in 1989 one-third of their exports were sold to each other, compared with one-quarter in 1979.

Table 3: Britain's Trade with Africa 1991

	£m
Exports	
Sub-Saharan Africa	2,778.4
Commonwealth	1,405.9
South Africa	1,023.6
North Africa	790.2
Imports	
Sub-Saharan Africa	2,148.4
Commonwealth	999.6
South Africa	954.8
North Africa	573.6

For historical reasons, most of Britain's trade with Africa is with Commonwealth countries and South Africa. In 1991, Britain's export trade to Commonwealth countries in Africa totalled

£1,405.9 million, including £544.6 million to Nigeria, £206.9 million to Kenya and £135.3 million to Zimbabwe. British exports to South Africa totalled £1,023.6 million in 1991. Imports from the Commonwealth African countries totalled £999.6 million, including £250.2 million from Mauritius, £249.5 million from Nigeria, £142 million from Kenya and £103.8 million from Zimbabwe; imports from South Africa were £954.8 million. In 1991 Britain's main trading partners in Africa outside the Commonwealth (excluding South Africa) were Algeria, Egypt and Morocco.

European Community

Britain has been a member of the European Community since 1973. The Community is the world's largest trading unit and acts on behalf of its member states in most international trade negotiations, some of which are significant for Africa, including 16 Commonwealth countries there.

Lomé Convention

During the negotiations for Britain's accession to the Community in the early 1970s, the Government was concerned that its membership should not be detrimental to Commonwealth states in Africa, the Caribbean and the Pacific, and that the interests of those countries dependent on the export of certain commodities should be safeguarded. The Treaty of Accession therefore offered 20 independent Commonwealth countries several forms of relationship with the enlarged Community, one of these being to join with existing associate countries in negotiating an agreement covering both trade and aid. This was accepted by a number of the developing countries and resulted in the signing of the first Lomé Convention in 1975 between the European Community and 46 countries in Africa, the Caribbean and the Pacific (known as the ACP countries). There are now 69 ACP signatories, about half of whom are members of the Commonwealth.

The Convention provides for the duty- and quota-free entry into the Community market of most agricultural products imported from the ACP signatories, and all industrial products (except rum). There are special protocols to safeguard the interests of those ACP countries dependent on the export of such agricultural products as sugar, bananas and beef.

Under Lomé, the ACP countries are provided with a system of compensation against shortfalls in their export earnings from nearly 50 agricultural commodities (principally cocoa, coffee, groundnut products and cotton). The system applies to the earnings from an ACP state's exports of an eligible product, on condition that these represent at least 5 per cent of total earnings from exports of goods. For the least-developed, landlocked and island ACP states the percentage is 1 per cent. The Lomé Convention has a special fund providing loans at low interest rates for mining industries in difficulty. The fund can be used to improve the viability of those industries and to broaden the basis of the country's economic growth. The minerals covered include copper, phosphates, manganese, bauxite and alumina, tin and iron ore.

The current Convention (Lomé IV) runs for ten years to 2000, with financial resources provided by two European Development Funds on a five-year basis. Rural development and improved access for a range of agricultural products will continue to be the most important area of assistance under Lomé IV, but it also puts increased emphasis on the development of processing and manufacturing industries and the encouragement of activities in the private sector. Assistance will also be available in the form of finance for import programmes.

Generalised System of Preferences

The European Community's Generalised System of Preferences Scheme[3] is designed to increase the export earnings of developing countries, promote their industrialisation and accelerate their rate of economic growth.

The scheme provides duty-free entry for industrial products and preferential entry for a limited range of agricultural products, mainly processed products. The least-developed countries have special arrangements for such products, allowing duty-free access or specially reduced rates of duty

Almost all industrial products are granted duty-free access, but some quantitative limits are applied for certain products from the most advanced developing countries. The poorest countries are exempted from such restrictions and are granted special treatment for most agricultural products.

Other Support

To assist trade between Britain and Africa, support is given by government and government-funded organisations to help both British exporters and African countries importing their goods, and African exporters in finding markets in Britain.

Export Credits Guarantee Department (ECGD)

Since 1919 ECGD has been helping British exporters overcome many of the risks in selling overseas.

---

[3]Similar preferential trade schemes are operated by the major industrialised countries.

Following the privatisation of its short-term business in 1991, the department's principal role is the insurance of medium- and long-term credits for project-related exports. It also provides insurance for new investments against the risks of expropriation, war and restrictions on payments to Britain for goods and services. ECGD is responsible to the President of the Board of Trade.

Business which ECGD has supported includes:

—a £30 million line of credit to South Africa in response to a growing demand for British capital equipment;

—a £15 million line of credit to Ghana to finance the sale of capital plant and equipment;

—a £3 million line of credit to Zimbabwe to finance the sale of capital goods and associated services; and

—a £49 million loan as part of a £600 million project for the first phase of the construction in Lesotho of the highest dam in sub-Saharan Africa and attendant tunnelling; the project is also funded by, among others, the Commonwealth Development Corporation—some £21 million—and the World Bank—$110 million.

Overseas Trade Service
Assistance to British firms exporting to Africa is also given by the Government's Overseas Trade Service, which is advised by the British Overseas Trade Board (BOTB).

The Commonwealth and Africa

Commonwealth Secretariat

Of the 50 member states of the Commonwealth, 16 are situated in Africa. The Commonwealth is not exclusively concerned with consultations between governments; it also provides a forum for a large number of unofficial organisations which maintain contact on subjects such as sustainable development, the environment, health, law, women's development, and education. Intergovernmental consultations are organised by the Commonwealth Secretariat, which is 30 per cent funded by Britain (some £2.6 million in 1992–93), the rest coming from the other Commonwealth governments. The Secretary-General is Chief Emeka Anyaoku of Nigeria, who took office in 1990.

Biannual meetings of Commonwealth heads of Government and other ministerial meetings are held to discuss international developments and consider ways in which co-operation between members can be improved. The most recent meeting of heads of Government took place in Harare in October 1991 where they discussed democracy and human rights, the environment, progress towards political pluralism in South Africa and the lifting of sanctions, and debt relief. The meeting culminated in a statement of Commonwealth philosophy for the 1990s.

Relevant problems to African countries—moves towards multi-party democracy, international debt, the launching in 1990 of the Commonwealth Equity Fund designed to ease the flow of private institutional investment to Commonwealth developing countries, and the relationship between development and environmental issues—were discussed at other Commonwealth ministers' conferences, including the meetings of ministers of finance (October 1991) and agriculture (November 1991). At the finance meeting, ministers agreed to promote:

—assistance to governments for effective administration and the strengthening of democratic institutions;

—services to governments to develop market institutions and a larger role for the private sector; and

—advice and assistance in the development of capital markets, privatisation, and the promotion of investment.

The Commonwealth Secretariat also organises meetings, seminars and workshops throughout the Commonwealth. It co-ordinates agreed programmes of Commonwealth intergovernmental co-operation and provides technical assistance for economic and social development through the Commonwealth Fund for Technical Co-operation (CFTC). It also supplies member governments with a wide range of information and provides technical support to expert groups set up periodically by member states to report on major problems facing the Commonwealth.

The Commonwealth Fund for Technical Co-operation

Britain plays an active part in the work of the Commonwealth Fund for Technical Co-operation, established in 1971 as the operational arm of the Commonwealth Secretariat. It provides managerial, professional and technical assistance for economic and social development in Commonwealth developing countries. All members of the Commonwealth support the Fund, whose budget has grown from £400,000 in 1971 to £30 million in 1990–91. Canada (£8.6 million) and Britain (£7 million) made the largest contributions in 1990–91, followed by Australia, Brunei, India, New Zealand and Nigeria.

Under the Fund's General Technical Assistance Programme, experts working in such areas as education, public administration, finance and taxation, agriculture and rural development, industry, the environment, transport and communications, and legislation, are available at the request of governments in developing countries. In 1990 and 1991 technical assistance was given to more than 170 industrial projects and an estimated 7,000 jobs were created; projects in Africa and the Indian Ocean provided nearly 40 per cent of CFTC work.

The Fund is one of the pioneers of technical co-operation between developing countries and has always believed that expertise gained in one developing country is more easily applied in another. The majority of its experts and other personnel come from developing countries, and all its training, except in a few very specialised fields, takes place in institutions and workplaces in Commonwealth developing countries.

The Fund's Fellowships and Training Programme finances training for government middle-level personnel, managers and technicians. Courses cover such areas as nursing, librarianship, farm management, town planning, engineering, social welfare, meteorology, telecommunications, postal services, and customs and excise. In 1990 the Programme made training awards to around 4,700 people.

The Technical Assistance Group (TAG) provides consultancy advice in economics, law and computer systems in response to requests from member governments. It undertakes assignments in the fields of financial policy, including external debt-recording and management, and the development of natural resources and environmental projects. Following assistance from TAG experts in drawing up legislation, Namibia awarded its first oil exploration licence to a Norwegian consortium in April 1992; over the last two years, TAG has assisted other African countries in their petroleum negotiations, including The Gambia, Mozambique, the Seychelles, Tanzania and Zimbabwe.

The Industrial Development Unit (IDU) helps governments to plan new industries and to improve the performance of existing ones. Much of its work is with small- and medium-sized industries. It gives advice on matters such as energy conservation and renewable energy, waste recycling, environmental protection, pollution control and industrial safety. It also identifies investment opportunities, selects plant and facilities and helps with installation. Assistance to regional industrial co-operation programmes in Southern Africa, the Caribbean, and Asia and the Pacific is an important part of its work. The IDU has assisted a Kenyan tyre retreading company to expand into rubber reclamation by using redundant tyres; the new enterprise provides an income for the poor people who collect the waste tyres.

The Export Market Development Division promotes the export of commodities and manufactures through the following activities:

—market surveys, trade fairs and missions;

—assistance with product modification, design, packaging and standards; and

—training in marketing and trade negotiation.

It also organises conferences and other meetings and commissions research on trade and export matters important to Commonwealth developing countries.

It supports training courses, seminars, and workshops organised by other Secretariat divisions, in such fields as education, law, health, and science. A high priority was given during the Heads of Government Meeting in Harare to the advancement of women.

Through the CFTC, the Secretariat administers two special funds for Mozambique and Namibia. These were established at the request of the Commonwealth Heads of Government Meetings in 1987 and 1989 respectively. Started in 1988, the Mozambique fund is intended to run for five years. Its purpose is to mobilise resources; finance projects, for example in transport, communication and agriculture; support training; and build or strengthen bilateral and other contacts. To meet an acute skills shortage, the CFTC is providing technical assistance and training with a special focus on developing institutional capacity. Through its fund, Namibia has received help to restructure the public service and the education system, including, for example, the services of CFTC experts on school management and administration and youth development programmes.

The Commonwealth Nassau Fellowship scheme, in operation since 1986, is designed to promote the education of South African victims of apartheid. Through the multilateral part of the programme, which is financed by the Commonwealth governments with support from UN agencies and operated by the CFTC, the Commonwealth Secretariat provides awards for study at institutions mainly in Commonwealth developing countries. Some Commonwealth governments also offer Nassau Fellowships under bilateral arrangements. About 1,000 South Africans have received Commonwealth support under these schemes.

Commonwealth Secretariat and Democracy

Because of its neutral position, coupled with its commitment to democracy and human rights, the Secretariat is able to make its good offices available in cases of dispute and has carried out, on request, special assignments requiring impartiality.

In Africa, for example, the Commonwealth Secretariat organised a group of distinguished Commonwealth statesmen to observe the start of the Convention for a Democratic South Africa (CODESA) in Johannesburg in December 1991 (see pp. 46–7). Another Commonwealth group visited Namibia in September and October 1990 to observe the implementation of the independence process there. Independent Commonwealth parties organised by the Secretariat observed parliamentary elections in Zambia in 1991.

Together with the Secretariat's Legal Division, the TAG is also involved with requests from Commonwealth countries to assist in their transition to multi-party democracy. In 1980 Commonwealth technical teams and observers helped Zimbabwe in its transition to majority rule, and later in that year were present to oversee elections in Uganda. In 1989 technical experts from the CFTC helped in the drafting of Namibia's constitution, setting up administrative and trade union systems and drafting laws, while Commonwealth observers assisted in the independence elections. More recently, the Commonwealth Secretariat has been involved in the planning of multi-party elections in Mozambique, as well as in those promised in Lesotho and the Seychelles.

In March 1992 the Commonwealth Secretary-General partic-ipated in a high-level consultation on ways in which Africa and the international community can respond to internal conflicts in African countries; other issues discussed at the consultation included human rights and democracy, approaches to peacemaking and peacekeeping, and humanitarian assistance.

Britain and Southern Africa

For many years Britain has been concerned with the affairs of Southern Africa. Positive developments in the region since 1989 have included:

—a trend towards more accountable government and liberal economic policies with countries committed either to multi-party systems or to a greater degree of democracy; and

—steady progress towards non-racial democracy in South Africa.

Britain's policy towards South Africa, as outlined by Lady Chalker in a speech given in February 1992, is:

—to encourage all sides to conduct serious negotiations on a new constitution;

—to help end political violence and intimidation; and

—to persuade the international community to underpin South Africa's reforms by relaxing trade and financial sanctions, renewing South African access to the IMF and the World Bank, encouraging new investment, and giving targeted aid.

Lady Chalker said that elsewhere in the region Britain wanted:

—to help Zambia to develop IMF-backed economic reforms and to strengthen democracy;

—to contribute to the maintenance of peace in Angola, including the successful transition to multi-party democracy there, an economic reform agreement backed by the IMF, and greater British business interest in the country's development;

—to promote in Mozambique an early and full ceasefire, a durable peace agreement and the earliest possible elections under a multi-party system;

—to help Zimbabwe sustain successful economic reforms in conditions attractive to foreign investors;

—to improve respect for human rights in Malawi; and

—to encourage regional political co-operation and increase economic integration.

South Africa: Political Background

Reforms in South Africa since 1990 have included:

—the release of the African National Congress (ANC) leader, Mr Nelson Mandela, and other political prisoners;

—the lifting of the bans on the ANC and other political organisations;

—the lifting of the state of emergency and restrictions on the press; and

—the abolition during 1991 of crucial apartheid laws.

In December 1991 formal negotiations began between the South African Government and 18 other parties in the Convention for a Democratic South Africa (CODESA), in order to draw up a non-racial democratic constitution. Later, in March 1992, a referendum of white South Africans showed that a large majority (68 per cent on an 85 per cent turnout) wanted this process of constitutional reform to continue. CODESA has achieved agreement on a broad range of issues, both on the nature of the new constitution and on the arrangements for governing the country in the interim. But the parties continue to discuss other fundamental points such as constitutional protection for minority groups. Other questions, in particular the role of the security forces in the continuing violence in South Africa, led to the halting of the CODESA negotiations for a period.

International Reaction

Britain and the EC have consistently encouraged the CODESA process and taken steps to restore sustainable economic growth in South Africa. The Community's special programme for black South Africans continues to grow (Britain's contribution now stands at £7.5 million), while the EC's economic sanctions have gradually been removed. Britain believes that military sanctions, such as the UN arms embargo, should stay until the new constitution is in place. The United States, Japan and many other countries have similarly responded to reforms in South Africa by removing economic sanctions.

The Commonwealth countries at their October 1991 Heads of Government Meeting in Harare agreed:

—to continue to work to establish a free, democratic, non-racial and prosperous South Africa; and

—to remain ready to assist the negotiating process there.

Other conclusions of the Commonwealth meeting provide for:

—the retention of the UN arms embargo (established in 1985) until a post-apartheid South African Government is firmly established;

—the lifting of financial sanctions when there is agreement on the text of a new democratic constitution;

—trade and investment sanctions to be lifted 'when appropriate transitional mechanisms' have been agreed that will enable all the parties to participate fully in the constitutional negotiations;[4] and

—immediate suspension of consular and visa restrictions, cultural and scientific boycotts, and the restrictions on tourism.

The Commonwealth's Gleneagles Agreement of 1977 was effective in contributing to the sporting isolation of apartheid South Africa. In Harare in 1991, Britain and the other Commonwealth countries welcomed the International Olympic Committee's decision to allow South Africa to compete in the Olympic Games after the formation of a non-racial Olympic Committee there. Britain, other EC and Commonwealth countries and the international community at large believe that contacts should resume with those sports in South Africa which have achieved proper racial integration and unified governing bodies. The new non-racial United Cricket Board of South Africa has been admitted to the International Cricket Council, opening the way for South African participation in top international games; a South African team participated in the cricket world cup in 1992. The first of the 1992 Grand Prix motor racing series was held at Kyalami, South Africa, in February 1992. Also in 1992, South Africa returned to international rugby.

British Aid

Britain's expenditure on assistance for black people in South Africa during 1991 was around £10 million with a further £7.5 million as Britain's share of EC aid. Support covered:

[4]The European Community lifted the oil embargo in April 1992; earlier, the Community agreed in principle to lift bans on the import of iron and steel and on gold coins; a voluntary ban on new investment was lifted in December 1990.

The Commonwealth Development Corporation collaborates with private sector projects like those pictured here, helping to promote economic development through investment.

The Sheraton International Hotel, Gaborone, Botswana.

The Botswana Telecommunications Corporation.

The East Usambara Tea Co. Ltd.

British aid policy aims to help achieve sustainable economic growth by supporting well-designed development projects and helping to finance programmes aimed at strengthening educational institutions and systems.

Below: villagers in Chad being trained in handpump maintenance by the UN Development Programme.

The Overseas Development Administration (ODA) has assisted with the rehabilitation of the Limpopo Railway, Mozambique.

A British Council library in Kenya.

It is estimated that women are responsible for 80 per cent of agricultural production in Africa. Emphasis is being placed on improving their business skills, literacy and health care.

An ante-natal clinic in Uganda, funded by Oxfam.

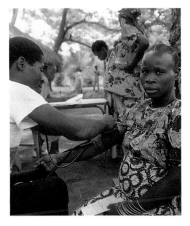

A fashion design, production and export business set up in Uganda with an ODA loan.

Making ceramic stoves in Kenya. The Intermediate Technology Development Group (ITDG) helps to develop small-scale technologies which will increase the income and skills of poorer sections of the community.

Importance is placed on improving methods of food production and animal husbandry.

Samburu herders in Kenya learning to give correct dosages of medicines to animals, with the help of the ITDG.

Sowing seeds, Ségou, Mali.

A VSO worker (see p. 26) with a farmer and colleague in Uganda.

—around 1,200 black South Africans in higher education, including over 600 financed in universities and technical colleges in South Africa under the British Awards Scheme;

—Nassau awards (60 in 1992–93) for one year's postgraduate study in Britain;

—a contribution of £75,000 for Nassau awards administered by the Commonwealth Fund for Technical Co-operation (CFTC);

—over 160 CFTC awards in 1991 for study in Britain between three months and one year;

—contributions to the United Nations Education and Training Programme for Southern Africa and to the Commonwealth Scholarships for Black South Africans Programme;

—Helen Suzman awards (including up to 20 awards a year for black women to study at the University of Witwatersrand); and

—some 75 British Council fellowships and visitorships.

Britain also provides substantial financial support for technical co-operation projects to improve primary and secondary education for black South Africans. Two projects (£1.85 million over four years) are designed to improve the quality of mathematics and science teaching; another (costing £600,000 over four years) is aimed at teaching basic literacy to black South African primary schoolchildren; a further project (£1.25 million over six years) to improve the quality of English language teaching began in 1990. Britain is also financing over 300 community development projects in addition to developing programmes in the health, urban and rural sectors.

Other Southern African Countries

Britain and other Commonwealth countries provide substantial support for the Southern African Development Co-ordination Conference (SADCC). Britain also recognises the key role that the organisation will continue to play in the development process in Southern Africa.

Founded in 1979, SADCC aims to promote regional economic development, communications and trade between countries. The ten members—Angola, Botswana, Lesotho, Malawi, Mozambique, Namibia, Swaziland, Tanzania, Zambia and Zimbabwe—have agreed in principle to admit South Africa as its eleventh member when a new non-racial, fully democratic government is in place.

Since 1981 Britain has contributed £1,157 million in bilateral aid to individual SADCC states, and has also given strong support to SADCC regional projects, largely concerning transport. British pledges to SADCC total £80 million to date.

Britain also contributes to SADCC and its members through the European Community which provided nearly £100 million between 1986 and 1990; Britain contributed £16.4 million, as well as around one-fifth of Community food aid to the region.

Britain is also providing security assistance to several states in the region as well as Namibia (see p. 51). In 1989–90, for example, British military personnel were involved in training troops in Lesotho, Swaziland and Zimbabwe, while students from these countries and from Malawi, Botswana and Tanzania attended military colleges in Britain. Britain is also training Mozambican soldiers. In 1990–91, 60 per cent of Britain's overseas military assistance went to Southern Africa.

The Commonwealth Secretariat supports SADCC by funding training, providing assistance in planning projects, consultancy advice, supplying technical experts and helping to set up new industries.

Namibia

Following elections in November 1989 supervised by the United Nations, a new assembly adopted in February 1990 a constitution for an independent Namibia. When Namibia became independent in March 1990, it joined the Commonwealth.

Britain provided a signal unit and a number of monitors to supervise the elections. At independence Britain pledged £10 million of aid over three years. The main focus is on education, other priority areas being police training, assistance with public service reform, health and agriculture. Outside the aid programme Britain is helping to train the Namibian army.

Education

Britain recognises the value of education in developing countries which is vital to improving the quality of human life and for the promotion of sustainable development. British bilateral aid finances a range of projects designed to strengthen educational institutions and systems. ODA assistance builds on local expertise and resources. This aid includes support for study fellows in Britain and overseas, for British teachers and other educationalists serving in developing countries, and for the provision of books and equipment for educational institutions. Other aid involves capital projects to provide for the construction and improvement of educational buildings and for equipment. Most assistance goes to developing countries in the Commonwealth. In these countries English is often the language of instruction for secondary and higher education. With a view to helping the poorest communities, a substantial proportion of aid is being directed to improving basic and non-formal education in rural areas.

Special attention is also given to:

—the development of technical and vocational skills;

—the reform of curricula with reference to local needs;

—the provision of books and the local production of cheap educational materials and equipment;

—educational research; and

—the training of teachers and teacher trainers, educational planners, administrators, inspectors and advisers.

In Tanzania, assistance is being provided to help improve competence in the English language as the medium of instruction in secondary schools; between 1986 and 1991 over 100 Government, and nearly 130 private, secondary schools were helped. A system of training in all districts was established. Another five-year project has been approved to consolidate this development.

In Swaziland support has been provided to the College of Technology for technician and craft training and a longer support project is planned for a three-year period.

In Nigeria four polytechnics are receiving British help in order to improve the teaching of practical subjects by means of training workshops in technology teaching and equipment installation. The total cost of the aid is nearly £1.5 million for the period from 1989 to 1994.

In 1990 the number of publicly financed British people (including volunteers) engaged in education in over 50 developing countries was nearly 1,500. Most were working in secondary and further education (including teacher training) and especially in the teaching of English, mathematics, science, and technical and vocational subjects.

The British Government's general policy towards overseas students is that they should pay the full cost of their education in Britain. Although the majority of overseas students, with the exception of those from the European Community, pay their own fees and expenses or hold awards from their own governments or other sponsors, the British Government continues to make provision for most students from developing countries.

As part of Britain's aid programme to developing countries in 1990–91, the ODA supported 15,886 students (10,034 of these were from Commonwealth countries) in Britain.

Information

Access to information in its written form is an essential element in the transfer of skills, and books continue to be the most immediately accessible medium in which information can be kept. For developing countries, Britain provides books (in Africa often through 27 British Council libraries) or advice through training and other forms of know-how which can develop local people's own publishing skills. Britain also supports distance education activities through the Commonwealth of Learning by providing finance (£2 million over five years) to the International Centre for Distance Learning at the British Open University for the development of a database.

To help the supply of books to developing countries, the ODA funds or co-funds studies to examine the particular situation in each recipient country. Each study highlights problems facing the production and supply of books, and provides possible areas of investment in the future. The studies cover, among other things, cultural needs, raw material, printing and production, authorship, publishing, marketing, distribution, and financing. A number of studies have been carried out in Sierra Leone (1987), Tanzania (1989), Nigeria (1990) and Kenya (1991).

However, the shortage of textbooks and reference books in many African institutions is still providing a serious constraint on access to knowledge and education at all levels. To assist in overcoming this shortage, the ODA has supported a number of book projects in Africa. In October 1991, the ODA and the British Council sponsored a conference in Manchester on textbook provision and library development for African ministers of education.

The Educational Low-Priced Book Scheme makes available to students and libraries specially selected British textbooks in 86 developing countries. A subsidy by the ODA of £1.2 million in 1991–92 enables books to be priced at between one-third and one-fifth of the cheapest standard British editions. There are some 500 titles covering science, technology, medicine, nursing, veterinary science, agriculture, business and English-language teaching.

The ODA also helps the largest book-aid charity, the Ranfurly Library Service (RLS), with an annual grant—some £60,000 in 1991. The RLS provides around 750,000 books per year for educational institutions, libraries and communities in some 70 developing countries. In one of the charity's book buying projects—it bought £250,000-worth of books in 1990—the RLS provided a primary school for the deaf in Kenya with specialised teaching materials. To support local publishing the RLS is working on a project to distribute African published books to universities and children's libraries. Also the ODA made a contribution (£186,000) to the 'Textbook for Africa' project through which thousands of textbooks no longer required in Britain were despatched over three years.

In Sierra Leone, the ODA established a textbook development project which included the provision of cheap and durable textbooks for primary school children in English, mathematics, social studies and science. Local authorship and editing skills were combined with British publishing expertise to develop and produce pupils' texts, teachers' books and supplementary materials for every primary school in the country. As a result of the project the ratio of textbooks to pupils was reduced from 1:100 to 1:2.5, at a cost of 75 pence per pupil.

The ODA donated two fully-equipped mobile library vans to The Gambia. The vans provide library books for children and adults who live in remote rural areas.

The British Council

Much of Britain's educational aid is provided through the British Council, which administers certain programmes on behalf of the ODA. In 1990–91 Africa was the largest sector of the Council's expenditure (28 per cent, nearly £100 million).

The British Council is Britain's main agent for cultural relations overseas. It is financed largely from grants from the Government (including the ODA); most of its budget is devoted to education in the widest sense. The Council has five main activities:

—helping people to study, train, or make professional contacts in Britain;

—enabling British specialists to teach, advise or establish joint projects abroad;

—providing library and information services overseas;

—promoting British education, science and technology; and

—making British arts and literature more widely known.

During 1991, the Council started a public-sector financial management training programme in Tanzania and supported a forestry teaching and research scheme in Kenya; it also opened libraries and English Language Teaching resource centres in Maputo (Mozambique) and Bulawayo (Zimbabwe).

Higher Education

The Council manages an ODA-funded (£3.4 million in 1991–92) programme of academic links between British universities and polytechnics and those in developing countries. Some are collaborative (in Egypt, for example) while others provide special expertise. Newcastle University's School of Architecture, for example, has links with institutions in Nigeria, Kenya and Ghana, the aim being to create teams of architects, planners and technicians capable of implementing a national housing development policy.

As part of a four-year, £1.6 million agreement between Rank Xerox and the Council, students from eight African countries came to Britain in 1990 in a fellowship programme. The Council is also assisting the University of Sierra Leone to develop and expand, bringing in external examiners and visiting lecturers, and training staff, as well as other programmes such as book presentations, short-term visits and long-term scholarships.

Civil Service Training

The Council is currently managing a number of ODA-funded projects designed to support the development of civil service and local government systems overseas. These include a training development programme for the office of the Head of the Nigerian Civil Service; the strengthening of audit capabilities and financial and personnel management in the Tanzanian civil service; and in Uganda a £1.9 million project to improve the policy-making, leadership and management skills of senior civil servants.

In 1989 the Council was asked to provide experts to help in Sierra Leone's plans to decentralise local government, in particular in the fields of training of newly elected councillors, management, finance, and personnel recruitment. The Council is continuing its involvement by strengthening existing contacts with British local authorities and through a phased programme of exchange visits, specialised training courses in Britain, and support to in-country training programmes.

English Language Teaching

The Council co-ordinates the provision of English language specialist services from Britain. In Commonwealth countries much of this takes the form of ODA-funded projects supporting wider aid objectives. In Zambia the Council is helping to raise the level of English language competence in primary and secondary schools. In South Africa, new ODA-funded projects began in 1991, including English teaching at secondary level and early-learning activity.

Books and Information

The provision of access to British books, periodicals and professional journals has always been one of the Council's main tasks. It runs 144 libraries and information centres throughout the world, handling over 8 million issues a year. In sub-Saharan Africa, the Council has 27 libraries with over 121,500 members. The libraries provide information on British educational practice, the role of women in development, the promotion of economic reform, and British experience and practice in environmental, health and population issues. Many of the Council's projects involve collaboration with the World Bank and other international donor or lending organisations, covering support for manpower training, book and periodical collection, library automation, planning and management.

A major Council-funded conference in Nigeria to publicise and present the result of a World Bank/ODA Book Sector Study led:

—to the redrafting of the Nigerian National Book Policy;

—to changes in import regulations for book-related materials; and

—to changes in the design of a $120 million World Bank education project.

In Ethiopia, to avoid overcrowding in its Addis Ababa library, the Council organised a bulk loan scheme in which the Council distributed over 10,000 textbooks to twenty-five secondary schools in the capital.

The Commonwealth Institute

The Commonwealth Institute in London is an independent organisation—substantially financed by the British Government—and is the centre of Commonwealth education and culture in Britain. Commonwealth countries are represented through a programme of permanent and temporary exhibitions. Among the other facilities provided are two art galleries, a theatre, an Information Centre, teaching and education services for schools and adult groups, a commercial picture library and a shop stocking crafts and resource materials.

The Commonwealth Resource Centre contains information on Commonwealth countries (including those in Africa), peoples and organisations. A loans collection is available to schools and other education institutions in Britain; this includes literature, audio-visual materials and information books. Resource packs can be hired. The reference collection provides journals, press cuttings, directories and yearbooks.

The Institute has helped to develop the new national school curriculum in England and Wales and provides teachers in its support. Educational services include consultancies, workshops, conferences, festivals and special holiday activities for children. The Institute also supports the Commonwealth of Learning (see p.54) and works closely with other Commonwealth countries in its educational and cultural activities.

The Commonwealth Institute, Scotland, aims to further a knowledge and understanding of the Commonwealth and its member states through close co-operation with Scottish schools, universities and colleges of education. It works in primary schools and provides resources in the form of publications, conferences and exhibitions. It also contributes to curriculum design and development.

Broadcasting

The British Broadcasting Corporation (BBC) World Service provides some 140 hours of radio broadcasts a week across Africa, which are heard by an estimated 26 million people (i.e. people who listen at least once a week). Its main objectives are to give unbiased news, to reflect British opinion and to project British life, culture and developments in science and industry. The output includes news bulletins, current affairs programmes, political commentaries, topical magazine programmes, a sports service, music, drama and general entertainment. It is planned that BBC World Service Television, launched in 1991 and currently covering Europe, the Far East and Africa will be extended world-wide by 1993.

BBC African Service

BBC African Service, the oldest pan-African broadcasting network in the world, was established in 1940 to provide radio programmes in English. The service was expanded in 1957 to give programmes in Hausa, Somali, and Swahili. Its programmes range from:

—a breakfast radio show entitled Network Africa featuring news, sport, music and comment;

—*Focus on Africa*, an up-to-the-minute news programme;

—*African Perspective*, a serious weekly series analysing a major African issue; and

—*Spice Taxi*, a programme that looks at what makes life enjoyable in Africa.

The African Service has also launched 'late night' programmes for listeners in South Africa on music, sport and general knowledge. In addition, the service publishes a quarterly magazine, called *Focus on Africa* which has a worldwide distribution of 47,000 (40,000 in Africa alone).

In 1960, the BBC French Service started special broadcasts to Africa in French; Portuguese programmes to the continent followed shortly after.

Links with Commonwealth Broadcasters

Britain maintains close contact with the broadcasting organisations in the African countries of the Commonwealth. These organisations used the model of the BBC in the setting up of their own national broadcasting systems after independence, helped by British grants, secondment of BBC staff and training of African staff in Britain.

The BBC is a member of the Commonwealth Broadcasting Association, whose members extend to each other such facilities as the use of studios, recording channels and programme contributions.

The BBC continues to provide technical aid, particularly in training the staff of other broadcasting organisations throughout the world, and sends members of its staff overseas on training and consultancy visits. The Government finances overseas students on broadcasting training courses run by the BBC, the British Council and the Thomson Foundation.

The BBC also operates a unit which is the most extensive language-teaching scheme in the world; lessons in English are broadcast daily to most parts of Africa as part of its global coverage.

Health and Population

In 1990 Britain spent over £23 million on health and population related activities in Africa. The ODA aims to establish sustainable, effective, affordable and appropriate health services for the benefit of the poorest people. Assistance is focused on the health of women and children, family planning, and services preventing disease and disability. Britain is concentrating on assistance to 22 priority countries, mainly in Africa and South Asia.

Health

In Ghana, Kenya and Zimbabwe, Britain is helping to improve the organisation, management and financing of health services. In other African countries primary and district health care services are being strengthened. Particular programmes include:

—malaria control in Kenya following the resurgence of chloro-quine-resistant strains and insecticide resistance in vector mosquitoes; and

—ODA-funded research by the London School of Hygiene and Tropical Medicine, in collaboration with the University of Kumasi, Ghana, to monitor the incidence of ill-health associated with vitamin A deficiency in children, and the effectiveness of supplementation projects.

The ODA also helps to fund the considerable health and population assistance provided by the European Community, the UN Children's Fund, the World Bank, the regional development banks and British NGOs.

AIDS

AIDS continues to spread rapidly worldwide. The World Health Organisation (WHO) estimated in December 1991 that there were 2.5 million cases of AIDS. It predicts that by 2000 there will be 12 to 18 million AIDS cases and some 30 to 40 million cases of infection by the human immunodeficiency virus (HIV), the causative agent of AIDS. The disease is having an increasingly severe impact on certain developing countries, particularly in Africa, where about 6.5 million people (including nearly 1 million children) are carrying HIV. The highest number of cases there occurs in the 20–39 age group—those in their most economically productive years. The impact has been exacerbated by poverty and a lack of basic medical and administrative infrastructure.

International efforts to counter HIV and AIDS are co-ordinated by the WHO's Global Programme on AIDS (GPA), established in 1987. Up to September 1991, the GPA had received over $275 million in donor contributions for its central funding budget, making it the biggest UN health programme.

Britain is the third largest donor—more than £26 million to date—to the WHO's Global Programme on AIDS. It has also pledged:

—£8.2 million to 17 WHO national programmes to control the disease in Africa, Asia and the Caribbean;

—£3 million for research into the demographic and socio-economic aspects of AIDS; and

—a £3 million grant to the London-based International Planned Parenthood Federation (IPPF) to help family planning associations to develop their AIDS-related work.

Britain is also giving £4.7 million as part of its share of the European Community's AIDS programme for developing countries under the EDF.

Population

The world population has doubled since 1950 at an annual rate of 1.7 per cent; of the 90 million people added to the global population each year, 85 million are in developing countries. The greatest increase has been in Africa, where the population growth rate is about 3 per cent.

High population growth rates will prevent many developing countries from achieving sustainable development and alleviating poverty, and reduce the chances of improving women's and children's health. Britain therefore emphasises population as a priority within its aid programme: spending on population activities has grown fourfold since 1951 to a total of over £26 million in 1991. ODA support is concentrated on improving access to family planning, improving service quality and strengthening programme management.

The 'Children by Choice not Chance' initiative, launched by the ODA in August 1991, placed special emphasis on increasing bilateral population assistance, with a major focus on five African countries (Kenya, Malawi, Nigeria, Tanzania and Uganda).

However, the major share of Britain's population aid will continue to be grants to the multilateral population agencies: the United Nations Fund for Population Activities (UNFPA), IPPF, and the WHO's Human Reproduction programme. In 1991, ODA support for these agencies totalled more than £17.5 million; in 1992 it increased to £19.75 million.

Under the Joint Funding Scheme the ODA meets 100 per cent of the cost of population projects run by non-governmental organisations. Spending under this scheme has increased from £87,000 in 1987 to nearly £1 million in 1991.

Research

The ODA supports health and population research in Britain and overseas which helps developing countries to tackle health conditions. As well as helping to finance the activities co-ordinated by the Tropical Medicine Research Board of the Medical Research Council, the ODA is providing £16 million over a five-year period for a series of major new research and training programmes at the Liverpool and London Schools of Tropical Medicine. The ODA is contributing to WHO special programmes in the fields of tropical diseases, AIDS, human reproduction, diarrhoeal diseases, acute respiratory infection, essential drugs and drug abuse.

It also helps to fund the considerable health and population assistance provided by the European Community, the UN Children's Fund, the World Bank, the African Development Bank and British non-governmental organisations.

Women and Development

Special attention is given to the needs of women in all Britain's aid activities. A main priority is greater access to basic education, especially to literacy. Limited access to education hinders women's effectiveness in achieving improvements in health, agriculture (the Food and Agriculture Organisation—FAO—has estimated that women are responsible for 80 per cent of agricultural production in Africa), and family planning.

There are other obstacles impeding women's full participation in development.

—Poverty: in rural areas, the proportion of women in poverty has been increasing over the last 20 years, yet many are heads of households and most are farmers who provide 55 per cent of the food grown in the developing world.

—Legal restrictions: women are also prevented in some countries from owning land and assets, or from having bank credits to start small-scale businesses.

—Access to planning: in agricultural services, women have also had to follow advice or decisions provided mostly by or for men.

Projects in Africa

In *Nigeria,* a crop-protection training project to help women involved in field work and crop storage is designed to improve standards of training at village level. The project, which will benefit the poorer small-scale farmers, focuses on the role of women in crop

The Environment

Global environmental problems require an international effort to solve them. Britain believes that developing countries, which will be affected by climate change, ozone depletion and the loss of biological diversity, will have to participate fully in that effort, assisted by the development-aid donors.

Britain took an active part in the 1992 UN Conference on the Environment and Development (the Earth Summit) which took place in Rio de Janeiro in June 1992. The aims of the conference were to address the complex relationship between environment and development and to draw up a comprehensive action programme for international activity into the next century.

The main results of the conference were:

—a convention on climate change which commits countries to devise measures to combat climate change, including measures aimed at reducing emissions of carbon dioxide and other greenhouse gases to 1990 levels by the year 2000; and

—a convention on biological diversity, which requires countries, among other things, to identify and monitor important species and to set up networks of protected areas to safeguard them.

It is estimated that if the current rate of extinction continues, up to one-third of all species could be lost within the next 30 or 40 years, resulting in the loss of vital medicines and foods for the future. One of the reasons is human activity—partly over-hunting, poaching and illegal trade, and partly agricultural and industrial development. Britain considers that maintenance of habitats is the best way of conserving plant and animal species, and, in studying the environmental impact of new aid projects, encourages the restoration of habitats wherever possible.

Other results of the Earth Summit included:

—the Rio Declaration, a statement of principles, balancing environmental concerns with the need for development; and

—Agenda 21, a comprehensive action-plan for governments, international organisations, non-governmental organisations and others, covering over 40 different sustainable development programmes, mainly to assist developing countries.

Britain has already contributed £40.3 million to a new fund— the Global Environment Facility—set up by the World Bank and the United Nations in 1990 to help developing countries play their part in tackling global environmental problems. The British Government believes that the facility should assist developing countries in meeting their obligations under the two new environment conventions.

Britain is one of the largest contributors—£4 million in 1991—to the UN Environment Programme (UNEP), which co-ordinates environment issues within the UN system. The Government believes that UNEP has a major role to play in improving the international response to global and environmental threats and that it will need further strengthening to enable it to do this.

Britain is making sure that its projects and programmes in Africa are environmentally sound and sustainable while addressing local and national environmental priorities.

Kenya and Ghana have received British finance for studies on the impact of climate change on their countries. A policy for Zimbabwe also looked at the economic implications of limiting CO_2 emissions.

Another serious environmental problem is deforestation. Since its forestry initiative in 1988 to help developing countries to maximise the economic and social benefits from forest resources, Britain is now funding over 200 forestry projects at an estimated cost of £158 million.

In Africa these include:

—a forestry inventory and management project (part of a larger programme with the Ghanaian Government, the World Bank and the Danish International Development Agency), designed to improve the management, utilisation and conservation of the tropical high forest on a sustainable basis;

—conservation of genetic resources in Cameroon;

—assistance with forest inventory and management in the Oban hills of Nigeria; and

—small-scale bee-keeping in the forests of Tanzania.

In Egypt, the British Council has administered in collaboration with Suez Canal University and Portsmouth University an ODA-funded project on reed-bed sewage treatment. The result is a simple, inexpensive and environmentally safe method for the treatment of sewage to provide water for irrigation. Also, during 1989–91, the Council arranged 30 fellowships to enable Egyptian specialists to undertake training in Britain in environmental, pollution and conservation studies.

The Commonwealth and the Environment

In their 1989 Langkawi Declaration, Commonwealth leaders recognised the threat to the global environment and committed themselves to collective and national efforts of environmental conservation, as well as support for the Rio Earth Summit in 1992. The

1991 Commonwealth Heads of Government meeting promised special assistance to small Commonwealth member states to enable them to participate effectively in Rio. The Commonwealth Secretariat administers Langkawi training awards funded by Canada, to improve environmental skills.

The Secretariat and related agencies such as the Commonwealth Science Council (CSC) are implementing a number of initiatives to protect the environment and promote sustainable development. These include a 10-year CSC programme on renewable energy resources in Africa and a five-year Secretariat project to help African countries plan conservation strategies.

Country-level initiatives include water-plant control in Zimbabwe, small business and industrial pollution control in Nigeria, reclamation of used rubber tyres in Kenya, promoting butane gas rather than wood for fuel in The Gambia, and preserving coral sands in Mauritius. In The Gambia, the Secretariat has been assisting the government, other agencies and local people in tackling pollution and siltation of the river which supplies about half of the drinking water of Accra and downstream irrigation.

Private Sector

Private Investment

Britain is a major source of private investment going to developing countries, providing over £2,660 million in direct investment in 1990. This is as much as all the other EC countries combined.

British investment is encouraged through:

—the provision of export credits to support sound investment projects (the Aid and Trade Provision—ATP, see pp. 75);

—Government loans to the Commonwealth Development Corporation (CDC, see pp. 75–7) for investments in the private sector in the developing countries; and

—government insurance to investors by the ECGD (Export Credits Guarantee Department).

Other areas in which Britain has been assisting in private investment include its contributions to multilateral agencies—such as EC aid through the Lomé Convention, the World Bank and United Nations bodies.

Britain also supports the Multilateral Investment Guarantee Agency (MIGA) and more than 30 bilateral investment promotion and protection agreements with developing countries. They protect foreign investors against non-commercial risk and therefore remove one of the barriers to investment and private sector development.

The Commonwealth also encourages the development of private investment to developing countries. In September 1990 the

Commonwealth Equity Fund was launched, which is aimed at attracting private investment in emerging stock markets.

Aid and Trade Provision

Established in 1978, the Aid and Trade Provision (ATP) is designed to match the mixed credit practices of other donors by providing aid in combination with export credits to support sound projects offering commercial opportunities to British exporters. This aid benefits not only the countries to which it is given but also helps British companies win projects in developing countries. The budget for 1991–92 is £117 million.

Agreements concluded with African countries in 1991–92 involved the provision of funds for the Kotoka International Airport project and the Power V project in Ghana.

Commonwealth Development Corporation

Created by Britain in 1948, the Commonwealth Development Corporation (CDC) promotes economic development by investing in 48 developing countries. About 25 per cent of Britain's project aid—now £175 million a year—is being invested by the CDC; 70 per cent of investments are in Commonwealth countries.

Much of the Corporation's funding is in the form of Government loans at concessional rates allocated from the official aid programme. Increasingly, the CDC uses its own internally generated surpluses for re-investment. Some 63 per cent of CDC investments in 1991 went to private sector projects; in 1980 the proportion was only 30 per cent. Other sources include international aid agencies, agencies of other countries and local interests. Since 1987 the Corporation has sought to place at least:

—40 per cent of new commitments in projects which develop renewable natural resources (agriculture, forestry and fisheries); and

—30 per cent in basic infrastructure (power and water, telecommunications, housing, and transport).

The CDC's total investments and commitments at the end of 1991 were more than £1,331 million in 310 projects. Some 40 per cent of this—over £500 million—was in Africa: Central Africa £162 million, East Africa £142 million, West Africa £140 million, and Southern Africa £86 million. Between 1987 and 1991 new CDC commitments totalled £259.3 million.

Table 4: New CDC Investments in Africa, 1987 to 1991

£m

Sector	E Africa	C Africa	S Africa	W Africa	Total
Basic development	12.1	12.3	22.1	10.4	56.9
Primary production and processing	38.4	47	2.9	31.9	120.2
Finance, industry, and commerce	28.2	36.3	10.4	7.3	82.2
Total	78.7	95.6	35.4	49.6	259.3

Some of the recent projects undertaken by the CDC include:

—mixed farming and coffee, tea, and dairying (Malawi);

—pine and eucalyptus plantations (Swaziland);

—tannin-extract production forestry, hybrid maize, wheat and tea (Tanzania);

—commercial property and sugar production (Uganda); and

—coffee and mixed food crops and cattle ranching (Zambia).

Other commitments involve:

—finance to buy and install printing and packaging equipment (Cameroon);

—investment in a private pineapple plantation and export company (Ivory Coast);

—a merchant bank (Ghana);

—investment in the construction of a refinery to process crude tar and benzol (Zimbabwe);

—expansion of the smallholder tea development authority (Kenya);

—support for Swaziland's first stockbroking company;

—a cut flower project (The Gambia); and

—a seafood processing and marketing operation in Ghana.

The Crown Agents

The Crown Agents for Oversea Governments and Administrations is a statutory body providing financial, professional and commercial services for over 100 governments and 300 public authorities and international organisations; many of its clients are from Africa. Crown Agents does not receive any subsidy from public funds and is independent of any commercial interest in Britain or elsewhere.

The services provided by the Agents cover:

—the purchase, inspection and shipment of materials and equipment;

—supervision and management of supply, agricultural and engineering projects;

—money management and investment; and

—recruitment, consultancy and training.

Crown Agents plays a significant part in the administration and implementation of the British aid programme in Africa. Some of its projects during 1991 included:

—procurement deals for the Nigerian health sector through the British programme aid;

—ODA-funded projects in Kenya, Ghana, Malawi, Tanzania, Uganda and Zimbabwe; and

—buying equipment for the Limpopo railway link in Zimbabwe and for the Beira corridor and Nacala line in Mozambique.

Crown Agents is also involved in the work of international aid agencies (the United Nations, the European Development Fund and the World Bank, for example) and other countries' bilateral aid programmes. Under the second phase of Japan's non-project grant-aid programme, Crown Agents is managing procurement in 12 African countries (Burundi, Ghana, Guinea-Bissau, Malawi, Mozambique, Nigeria, Rwanda, Sierra Leone, Tanzania, Uganda, Zambia and Zimbabwe) at a value of more than £50 million. It also managed a veterinary drugs and vaccines aid programme in Ghana, funded by Germany. For the European Community, Crown Agents was involved with procurement projects in Zambia and supervision and technical assistance for a fertiliser buffer stock project in Malawi.

Recent training activities by the Crown Agents have included several courses on management of prisons, supplies and materials, and road maintenance. Training courses for customs officers have been run in Ghana and Uganda, and training courses in trade-fraud prevention provided in Lesotho. In Nigeria training programmes in site and maintenance management have been provided.

Research

There are a number of scientific research agencies responsible to the ODA which provide research resources to support practical development activity in Africa. The ODA also makes extensive use of the British research councils, universities and colleges, and other public and private research organisations, as well as international research bodies.

Natural Resources Institute

The ODA's Natural Resources Institute (NRI) collaborates with developing countries to increase the sustainable productivity of their renewable natural resources through the application of science and technology—for example, in the improvement of pre- and post-harvest technology of tropical crops, the utilisation of waste material and/or the promotion of non-timber forest crops. The NRI's main fields of expertise are resource assessment and farming systems; integrated pest management; and food science and crop utilisation.

The NRI aims to:

—carry out research and surveys;

—identify, prepare, manage and execute projects;

—develop pilot-scale plant, machinery and processes;

—provide advice and training; and

—publish scientific and development material.

The beneficiaries of the NRI's work are producers in the renewable natural resources sector, including agro-industrialists, and consumers. The main focus is on food crops consumed locally and on forestry and livestock, but work is also done on export produce such as cotton, fruit and vegetables, oilseeds, beverage crops and spices.

The NRI funds a Newcastle University team which studies the application of locally mined carbonatite as a cheap source of phosphate fertiliser in Malawi; it is also financing trials there following NRI-funded research at Reading University into the potential effectiveness of a bacteria as a control agent against root-knot disease in vegetables. In Togo and Kenya the NRI is involved in a major ODA-funded project to control the larger grain borer, a serious pest of maize and cassava in Africa.

Other examples of NRI's services include:

—setting up a computer network for the government of Zimbabwe;

—seconding publication specialists to a forestry project in Zimbabwe and to a livestock centre in Cameroon;

—conducting a study of the effects on fish of ground-spraying of DDT for tsetse fly;

—developing a new fuel-efficient kiln to smoke fish; and

—developing new ways to mill grain, thereby helping to increase farmers' incomes.

Though the practice of marine and freshwater aquaculture is active in South-East Asia, the possibility of developing this industry in Africa is only now being considered as a potential way for poor farmers to improve their food security. In view of the need for the new technology to fit into existing farming systems, and for a full understanding of the nature of the constraints and incentives facing farmers, an ODA-funded research project implemented by

Sussex University is to assess some of the social and cultural factors relevant to aquaculture development in Africa.

Through the SADCC, the ODA is also funding a major two-year investigation of the offshore ecology of Lake Malawi. The lake is said to provide about 70 per cent of the animal protein consumed in Malawi. One of the objectives of the investigation is to find out whether fisheries development would be economically viable.

CAB International

Britain is one of 29 member governments of CAB International which, since 1985, is open to countries outside the Commonwealth. It provides information, identification and biological control services for agriculturalists worldwide.

AFRC Institute of Engineering Research

Mainly funded by the ODA, the Overseas Division of the AFRC Institute of Engineering Research offers advice and technical assistance to developing countries on the engineering aspects of agriculture and rural development.

Overseas Development Institute

Founded in 1960, the Overseas Development Institute (ODI) is an independent centre engaged in development research on a wide range of issues which affect economic relations between North and South. It is a charity dependent on grants and donations from the British Government, commercial, voluntary and international organisations and the public. Many of the subjects researched in 1990–91 involve Africa, including:

—studies on food security and disasters;

—commercial change in pastoral Africa (funded by the ODA);

—the seed industry in Eastern and Southern Africa (part-funded by the NRI);

—the impact of structural adjustment programmes on African smallholders; and

—economic prospects for Zimbabwe.

International Research Centres

The ODA was a founder member of the Consultative Group on International Agricultural Research which was set up in the 1960s to support several international agricultural research centres focusing primarily on food crops and livestock production.

Forestry

The ODA has 40 tropical forestry research programmes as part of Britain's £160 million forestry initiative, announced at the United Nations in 1989; of 200 projects, 56 are being carried out by NGOs. The programmes cover:

—the role of trees and shrubs in agricultural systems, especially in maintaining soil fertility, preventing soil erosion, and providing fruits and fodder for livestock, and providing fuelwood;

—the inventory and management of natural forests, with a view to sustainable timber and non-timber production and conservation of tropical forest eco-systems; and

—the use of wood fuels, other products and agricultural residues for energy production.

ODA-funded research into non-timber production includes:

—edible and medicinal plants in Cameroon;

—bee-keeping in Tanzania; and

—mangroves in Guinea.

The ODA is giving Malawi money for the International Institute of Biological Control of CAB International to implement a five-year programme to find a natural enemy to aphids which are attacking new growth of cypresses and pines; these trees are an important element of the economy, generating paper pulp and timber for export and fuelwood for home consumption. Another research project started by the ODA in 1984 in Senegal is trying to develop species of sub-tropical fruits (particularly citrus fruits and bananas) that would help farmers to diversify their crops and boost their income. One large plantation, which produced 50,000 trees in 1990, now wants to build up a major export business.

The Oxford Forestry Institute manages an ODA-funded forestry research programme of 19 projects by other British universities and bodies such as the Royal Botanic Gardens at Kew and the Institute of Terrestrial Ecology at Edinburgh University.

Water Reserves

To counter the lack of rainfall and absence of underwater reserves in semi-arid areas, the ODA has been funding a ten-year research programme by the Institute of Hydrology and the British Geological Survey (both part of the Natural Environment Research Council), carried out in collaboration with a research station in Zimbabwe. By using wells with horizontal boreholes drilled out for distances of up to 40 metres, greater use could be made of local ground water supplies which are available at fairly shallow depths in a type of rock that occurs in large parts of Africa and elsewhere in the developing countries.

The ODA has also been supporting the work of the Institute of Hydrology in the Sahel region of Africa in developing effective soil and water management techniques and their implementation at farm level.

Abbreviations

ACP	African, Caribbean and Pacific (ACP countries)
ADB	African Development Bank
ADF	African Development Fund
AFRC	Agricultural and Food Research Council
AIDS	Acquired Immune Deficiency Syndrome
ANC	African National Congress
ATP	Aid and Trade Provision
BBC	British Broadcasting Corporation
BOTB	British Overseas Trade Board
CAB	Commonwealth Agricultural Bureau (formerly)
CAFOD	Catholic Fund for Overseas Development
CDC	Commonwealth Development Corporation
CFTC	Commonwealth Fund for Technical Co-operation
CODESA	Convention for a Democratic South Africa
CSC	Commonwealth Science Council
DAC	Development Assistance Committee
EC	European Community
ECGD	Export Credits Guarantee Department
EDF	European Development Fund
FAO	Food and Agriculture Organisation
GNP	Gross National Product
HIV	Human Immune Deficiency Virus
ICRC	International Committee of the Red Cross
IDA	International Development Association
IDU	Industrial Development Unit
IMF	International Monetary Fund
IPPF	International Planned Parenthood Federation
ITDG	Intermediate Technology Development Group
JFS	Joint Funding Scheme
MIGA	Multilateral Investment Guarantee Agency
NGOs	Non-Governmental Organisations
NRI	Natural Resources Institute
ODA	Overseas Development Administration
ODI	Overseas Development Institute
OECD	Organisation for Economic Co-operation and Development
RLS	Ranfurly Library Service

SADCC	Southern African Development Co-ordination Conference
SCF	Save the Children Fund
SPA	Special Programme of Assistance
TAG	Technical Assistance Group
VSO	Voluntary Services Overseas
UN	United Nations
UNEP	United Nations Environment Programme
UNESCO	United Nations Educational, Scientific and Cultural Organisation
UNFPA	United Nations Fund for Population Activities
UNHCR	United Nations High Commissioner for Refugees
UNPF	United Nations Population Fund
WHO	World Health Organisation

Further Reading

British Council Annual Report 1990–91.

British Overseas Aid: 1991 Annual Review. Overseas Development Administration.

Commonwealth Currents. Published free by the Commonwealth Secretariat every two months.

Commonwealth Development Corporation Report and Accounts 1991.

Commonwealth Development Corporation. A report by the Monopolies and Mergers Commission on the efficiency and cost of, and the service provided by, the Commonweaith Development Corporation. Cm 1983. HMSO, 1992, £15.80.

Commonwealth Secretary-General's Report 1991 (Commonwealth Secretariat).

Commonwealth Skills for the 1990s. The Commonweaith Fund for Technical Co-operation (Commonwealth Secretariat).

Crown Agents Annual Report and Accounts 1990.

Human Development Report 1990. United Nations Development Programme (Oxford University Press, 1992).

Index

Printed in the UK for HMSO.
Dd 0295908, 1/93, C30, 5673, 512423.

A MONTHLY UPDATE

ASPECTS OF BRITAIN

Current Affairs
a monthly survey

September 1992   Vol 22   No 9

London Conference on Former Yugoslavia
Outcome of the EC/UN Peace Conference

Balance of Payments 1991
Balance of Payments 'Pink Book'

Iraq
Deployment of Allied Military Aircraft over Southern Iraq

Research and Development
The Government's Annual Review of R & D

Regional Trends
Analysis of Regional Contrasts in Britain

CURRENT AFFAIRS:
A MONTHLY SURVEY

Using the latest authoritative information from official and other sources, *Current Affairs* is an invaluable digest of important developments in all areas of British affairs. Focusing on policy initiatives and other topical issues, its factual approach makes it the ideal companion for *Britain Handbook* and *Aspects of Britain*. Separate sections deal with governmental; international; economic; and social, cultural and environmental affairs. A further section provides details of recent documentary sources for these areas. There is also a twice-yearly index.

Annual subscription including index and postage £35·80 net. Binder £4·95.

Buyers of Britain 1993: An Official Handbook *qualify for a discount of 25 per cent on a year's subscription to* Current Affairs *(see next page)*.

HMSO Publications Centre
(Mail and telephone orders only)
PO Box 276
LONDON SW8 5DT
Telephone orders: 071 873 9090